How to Declutter Your Home for Simple Living

Decluttering Tips and Closet Organization Ideas for Creating Your Own Personal Oasis

(2nd Edition)

Judith Turnbridge

© 2012 Judith Turnbridge

All Rights Reserved. No part of this publication may be reproduced in any form or by any means, including scanning, photocopying, or otherwise without prior written permission of the copyright holder.

Disclaimer and Terms of Use: The Author and Publisher has strived to be as accurate and complete as possible in the creation of this book, notwithstanding the fact that he does not warrant or represent at any time that the contents within are accurate due to the rapidly changing nature of the Internet. While all attempts have been made to verify information provided in this publication, the Author and Publisher assumes no responsibility for errors, omissions, or contrary interpretation of the subject matter herein. Any perceived slights of specific persons, peoples, or organizations are unintentional. In practical advice books, like anything else in life, there are no guarantees of income made. This book is not intended for use as a source of legal, business, accounting or financial advice. All readers are advised to seek services of competent professionals in legal, business, accounting, and finance field.

First Printing, 2012

2nd Edition

Printed in the United States of America

Editor: Michael Bracewell

Table of Contents

The Home-Diet Plan 6

Does Having Clutter in Your Home Look Terrible? 8

How to Get the Motivation to De-clutter You Home and to Stop Always Putting It Off 13

How to De-clutter Your Home 15

De-cluttering Paperwork 17

The Easiest De-cluttering Method 20

The Living Room 22

The Kitchen 24

The Dining Room 27

The Bedrooms 30

The Bathroom 33

The Home Office 35

The Utility/Wash Room 38

Under the Stairs 39

The Garage 40

How to De-clutter a Small Apartment 42

How to Remove Anxiety and Stop Feeling Guilty When You've Thrown Your Things Away 44

How Many Clothes and Toys Do We All Really Need? 46

How to Teach Your Kids to De-clutter 48

How to Convince Someone Who Is a Hoarder to De-clutter Their Home 50

The Best Websites for Getting Rid of Your Home Clutter 52

How to Get a Tax Refund for Your Charity Donations 54

The 10-Minutes (or Less) Clutter-Free Action Plan 56

The Best Space-Saving Tips 60

Making Use of the Storage Area under Your Bed 62

Do Those Space Bags Really Work? 63

How to Clean and Organize Your Closet 64

How to Organize a Teen Girl's Closet 66

How to Build a Closet Organizer in a Closet with Dormered Walls 68

How Much It Approximately Costs to Have a Professional Design an Organized Closet 70

Simplicity and Harmony 71

About the Author 72

The Home-Diet Plan

…or How to De-clutter the Home So As To Have an Uncluttered Mind

Dealing with clutter in the home is something that most property owners will have to deal with at some point in their lives. It's a fact of nature that as we grow older we gather more possessions yet, for some reason, we decide against throwing out unwanted items and allow them to clutter-up our homes.

Clutter comes in many different forms; it can range from something as simple as unopened mail, newspapers and magazines, or come in the guise of an item you no longer use but feel may still come in handy one day. Alternatively, it may be something that you no longer like, but are reluctant to get rid of because it had cost so much or was something that was given to you as a gift. Finally, it could be a broken item that you never got round to fixing.

If clutter has built up, it is important to acknowledge that there is probably a reason for it. One good explanation I saw for this was, it being 'the result of choices' or, to put it another way, 'the choices you didn't make'. This means to de-clutter your home effectively, you are going to need to be ruthless with the decisions you make.

So far, you may be lucky and only suffer from clutter in the garage or shed, with the rest of your house remaining relatively clear, but ultimately you will have to address the issue. If not, the problem will only get worse. Eventually the lack of space in your outbuildings will result in other areas of your house becoming cluttered too.

The dictionary definition of 'clutter' is as follows:

> "an untidy collection of objects or disorganized mess"

However, there is more to clutter than just coming in the form of physical objects. Time and mental clutter can also cause problems. Time-clutter is caused when an individual has too much to do and not enough time in the day to do it. Mental clutter can often occur as a result of living a hectic lifestyle. The environment we live in can exacerbate these, so it is important to follow what our hearts are drawn to rather than surrounding ourselves with the things that we have kept for all the wrong reasons.

When embarking on any form of de-cluttering, you may feel intimidated by the task at hand, but this can be overcome by using the right approach. Before you start, it is best to spend a little time planning and preparing as this will avoid wasting time and effort on non-essential issues. A good starting point is to tackle one room at a time and then to set aside an allotted amount of time per day or week to deal with the task. I will talk in more detail about this later in the book, and I will even give you a plan of action that requires you to only spend 10 minutes or less on daily home organization.

Eventually when you start to see the benefits of de-cluttering, it will lead to a more relaxed atmosphere in the home. It will create a more organized environment where everything will have its place and you will no longer need to waste time looking for an item that you could never find before. A successful de-cluttering exercise will also result in a safer and healthier home because all the trip hazards will have been removed. Moreover, the lack of clutter will ensure housecleaning is easier too.

As the title of this chapter implies, many experts liken the de-cluttering process to going on a diet and similarly this process cannot be achieved overnight. It will take time, patience, and effort. Like dieting, the de-cluttering process involves making a plan and identifying and resolving bad habits, but it also acknowledges that a little bit of clutter can be acceptable occasionally.

So now, as you are about to embark on your home-diet program, I would like to encourage you with this inspiring motivational quote by Scott Reed:

"This one step – choosing a goal and sticking to it – changes everything."

Does Having Clutter in Your Home Look Terrible?

Hang on a minute! What's happening here? I thought you were on track to begin de-cluttering and now I'm hearing some 'ifs' and 'buts'. Well, don't worry because you're not alone with this.

The reason is, it's not uncommon to start making excuses for doing the job properly when you consider the amount and type of work involved. Let's take a look at two of the most common excuses and find out if they really are justified.

First Excuse: "Maybe having clutter in my home really doesn't look that terrible."

Answer: Having clutter in your home will not enhance the look of the house in anyway and will ultimately result in the house looking dirty and untidy. A cluttered home looks unpleasant and will eventually have a negative effect on you as a person. It may also cause problems with visiting friends and relatives as severe clutter may result in them feeling uncomfortable or forming negative opinions about you.

Second Excuse: "Maybe I'll just dump all my mess in one room and keep the door closed to the rest of the house."

Answer: Many homeowners who suffer from clutter will overcome the problem by dumping the mess in a particular room. Then they simply close the door to it, when guests arrive. When asked, they will claim that they will address the issue at a later date. This type of behavior is often known as procrastination, meaning "to delay doing something until later" and this can be a major barrier in the de-cluttering and reorganization process.

These, as well as the many other possible excuses we may have, are known as 'self talk' and can become a real hindrance towards completing our goal effectively. If you feel this relates to you, then start to become aware of these self-dialogues and notice the pattern they follow. Then turn them around to make them become productive dialogues. These will then empower you to overcome any doubts and unwelcome behavior; therefore, stopping procrastination. Remember, don't put off for tomorrow what you can do today.

Let's take a look at some other important issues which should also be addressed:

Storage

In order to maintain a clutter-free environment it is important that you have plenty of storage units available. Often, clutter is caused when a lack of suitable storage exists.

Sentiment

As I mentioned earlier, be ruthless when disposing of items that you no longer have a use for. If you are unsure about getting rid of something, consider the last time you used it. If you can't remember or you think it was over a year ago, then consider throwing it. On the other hand, if you are still unsure about the item then it might be worth storing it somewhere safe, such as in the loft or the garage, for a few months and then ask yourself the same question again. The chances are that if you have not bothered to retrieve the item since you originally put it there, then you don't need it, so it can be sold, thrown away, or recycled.

Time

Allow plenty of time so that you can reorganize properly. Only address one room or area because attempting to deal with more can be difficult and may not work. You don't want to become too overwhelmed by the task ahead of you.

Ask for Help

Enlist the help of other family/household members as the chances are they will be responsible for some or all of the clutter that has accumulated in the home. Openly encourage them to look after their own living space and ask them to help with keeping the shared areas of the house tidy.

Asking a friend to help can also be beneficial because they can look at the clutter objectively and without the emotional ties. They will then be able to give you some much needed advice and support. That's why they are often referred to as a "clutter buddy".

Stay on Top

Maintain good habits after the initial reorganization has happened, as it is important to remain on top of things and avoid returning to the bad, old ways. Ensure that every item has its own place and make sure it is returned to that when it's not being used.

Identifying the Cause of Clutter

An essential part of managing your clutter problem is to establish the reasons for its buildup. Once identified, you can then work at eliminating or correcting them. The chances are there could be some very simple reasons. A list of common problems are listed below.

Lack of Storage

If a lack of storage is the root of your problem, then this should be fairly easy to address. Before purchasing any storage, have a think about the things that need to be stored and consider the areas in which you will keep the storage containers.

Attitude

Sometimes a cluttered home is just a result of sheer laziness and a complete lack of motivation in addressing the problem. This type of behavior may not be associated with the person wanting to do the de-cluttering, but may relate to another household member.

Another Household Member

It is common to encounter problems with clutter when living with others because different people have varying degrees of tolerance towards this and untidiness. For families with children of a certain age, it may be necessary to educate the kids to understand what is expected of them. This is because they may not understand the concept of tidiness.

There may be a simple reason why another person in the house is causing the problem and providing a solution could benefit them greatly. For example, your partner may have developed a bad habit of leaving piles of clothes on the bedroom floor due to a lack of storage space in the closet. This could be because it is already full of your clothes and as a result, he has no other option. Therefore, the real cause of the problem isn't his sloppy behavior, it's because either the closet is too small or that you managed to fill it up with your own belongings. Therefore, it might be time for you to invest in more suitable storage or to have a clear out!

Children can be the cause of clutter with their toys and games being the source of the majority of problems. Whilst it would be unfair to expect a younger child to understand the concept of clutter, it can be a good idea to try to encourage them to clear away their toys after they have finished playing with them. Later in this book, I will give you some great tips for achieving this.

Lack of Time

If you feel that your situation was caused by a lack of available time to clear the mess, then it will be a case of having to prioritize and make the time available. If you feel that the task is too much for one person, then don't be afraid to ask for help and get a friend or relative involved to speed up the process. Remember your "Clutter Buddy".

If a lack of time is the source of the problem, then it may be worth looking at your lifestyle balance. You may be working too hard or socializing too much and not spending enough time organizing your home life.

Paperwork

A common source of clutter can come in the form of mail, newspapers, magazines, and old utility bills. A lack of filing space or a suitable storage area can often be the problem, so we will look at dealing with paperwork later in this book.

Taking the time to identify the cause of clutter in your home is an essential part of dealing with the problem because it allows you to address the issue from a broader perspective and to deal with the crux of the matter. This point may appear obvious, but is often overlooked. Too often that individual will rush into the task with the emphasis on clearing a room, but will not address the real problem of who or what has caused the mess in the first place.

…And now, as with being on any diet, the first thing you might lose is not those outdated kitchen utensils left to you by your elderly aunt, but in fact your sense of humor, so let's get ourselves some more motivation.

How to Get the Motivation to De-clutter You Home and to Stop Always Putting It Off

The start of any de-cluttering process will always be a daunting time. If your home is full of clutter, then it is perfectly understandable that you may be lacking the motivation to deal with the problem, but it is important to understand that it will not go away and will only get worse.

It is important to recognize that the reorganization process may take some time. It may take days or weeks depending on the severity of the problem, so before you start it's essential that you draw up a plan. Simply make a list of all the rooms in the house that need attention and note the problems within each room. This list can now be used as a useful motivational tool throughout the reorganization because it will give you the chance to tick off rooms when they have been completed. Tackle the problems in small bursts as many people find this technique works better for them.

Now that you have identified the issues that need to be addressed, it's just down to you as an individual to figure out how best to tackle the problem. As previously mentioned, some people prefer to do it a little at a time and not let it take over their lives, whereas other people will throw themselves into it and allocate a weekend or dedicate a number of days each week to resolve the issue.

There is no right or wrong way to approach the task and a lot will depend on your personality, but when drawing up your plan be honest with yourself and set yourself achievable targets and stick to them.

Consider the benefits of resolving the problem as a way of motivating yourself to start. Some of these benefits have been listed below:

– After reorganizing you will be able to locate things much easier and so will no longer find yourself wasting valuable time and getting stressed over looking for a particular item that you need.

– The home will be a safer place after it has been reorganized as clutter tends to create health and safety issues.

– Your home will become a healthier place because a clutter-free environment is easier to clean and will reduce the risk of allergenic problems that are caused by dust and the spread of germs.

– You may see a financial saving as a result of being more organized. Replacing items that you believed were lost will be a thing of the past and you will no longer incur late fees on bills because you will now have a new efficient filing system that keeps track on everything.

– Reducing the junk mail and receiving paperless statements will have a positive effect on the environment.

– You may even be able to recoup a little money on unwanted items by selling them at yard sales, through local advertisements, or on websites such as eBay. I will give you a full list of popular websites later in this book.

– Recycling old clothes and other unwanted articles can assist underprivileged people, so consider donating these to a local charity or worthwhile cause. In some instances, donating items can make you eligible for a tax deduction this can actually make you as much money as selling these articles but without the hassle. I will tell you more about this later!

– Finally, the biggest benefit should be the sense of achievement once you finally reach your goal. Be sure to maintain this by continuing to stay on top of the clutter. Then you can take the time to appreciate the uncluttered look of your home; the clear worktops, desktops, and dressers. Imagine that sense of calm when everyday you return to a tidy, organized home. Imagine that comfortable oozy feeling you will have in your own personal space as the stresses of everyday life pass away. Picture yourself with the freedom of flexibility. It will feel like a fresh ocean breeze has just swept over you.

De-cluttering is as much for the soul as it is for the home.

How to De-clutter Your Home

Now that we have a plan and have identified the areas that require attention, it is time to start the process of de-cluttering your home.

The first step is to establish where to begin. Depending on the amount of clutter, it might be worthwhile trying to tackle the most cluttered room first. Other people prefer to adopt a more methodical approach and to start with the downstairs living space and then work their way through the house. Whatever method you choose, it's important to note that you should only tackle one room at a time because any attempt to deal with multiple rooms will result in frustration and delays.

When you start the process, it is important to have a few things in place to help organize each room. When deciding on whether to keep something it may be useful to ask yourself the following questions:

Can the item be replaced if I need it at a later date?

Does the item improve my quality of life?

How often do I use it?

When do I use it?

When did I last use it?

Do I actually like it?

Does it actually work?

Make a note of these questions and then use them to assist with decision-making. Try putting a time limit on the amount of time you spend in each room, as this will help you to maintain your focus and work faster.

If you answered 'no' to the last question about whether the item works, then you will need to ask yourself why you are keeping it. If you intend on fixing it yourself, then set a time limit for doing this because many people will show good intentions, but will not actually get round to doing it.

One of the main reasons for clutter in the home is paperwork. Quite often piles of the stuff can be found everywhere. It can be piled-up in the entrance hall, on a kitchen worktop, on the dining room table, or even in the bedroom. Let's take a look at this first and then afterwards I will go on to show you a great fool-proof method for de-cluttering other household items.

De-cluttering Paperwork

The first thing that needs addressing is deciding on a designated area for papers, documents, mail, and receipts. Basically, anything that falls into this category should be placed there and dealt with accordingly.

When dealing with a mail problem it is important to recognize what type of mail is causing the problem. If you receive a large amount of non-essential junk mail, then consider contacting the companies that are responsible for sending it and ask them to remove you from their mailing list. You can also search "junk mail" on Google and this will return some alternative options for removing you from junk mail lists.

If the correspondence is not considered to be junk mail, then there are two options to consider.

Firstly, designate a place to keep your mail, such as a basket, shoe box, or bowl. This will ensure that you will always know where it is.

Secondly, you may want to set up some kind of basic filing system that allows you to store your most recent bills in a folder. Divide the folder into sections and use color-coding to keep them organized. Be aware that when using this option it's always a good idea to only keep recent bills. A 12-month history will be fine in most cases and a 13-tabbed file folder can be very good for doing this. You will have one pocket for each month, plus one spare.

I personally like to keep my bills for 12 months because I sometimes like to compare my most recent with a bill from the same time the previous year. Anything older than this should be destroyed, preferably by using a shredder because confidential documents should never be disposed of via the normal waste bin. If you are planning to buy a shredder, then go for a cross-cut model because these are the best.

Your tax return forms must be kept longer. The time can vary depending on the action, expense, or event the document records, but in most cases it should be for at least three years. In some circumstances, you may need to keep them even longer once the period of limitations has run out for the purpose of your insurance company or creditors. Visit the IRS website to find out more.

A great alternative for dealing with essential mail is to sign up for non-paper billings and automatic bill payments where possible. The majority of utility companies will have some kind of automated billing service on offer. This may come in the form of electronic statements, which are sent to you via email. Obviously, it is essential that you have a computer and email account before selecting this option.

Keeping a trashcan near to the door closest to the mailbox can also be very helpful. Then you can sort through your mail as you receive it and instantly toss away any unwanted items such as leaflets, unsolicited mail, and political campaign ads.

Receipts can be kept in a small plastic file with inserts to keep them separated. They can usually be tossed once you've checked your bank or credit card statement. The only times you might want to keep them for longer is if you are considering returning an item, if the item needs insurance valuation, or for tax purposes. Receipts could also be scanned and kept on a computer. Once again shred any receipts which might contain your full credit card information. You don't want to become a victim of identity theft.

Another common problem with paper-clutter can occur when old newspapers and magazines are kept. Be ruthless when dealing with this situation as it's unlikely that an old newspaper will have any value to you. Give magazines away to friends or libraries. If the reason for keeping them was that you were collecting a specific coupon or voucher, then simply cut the required item out of the paper and throw the rest.

If you do like to keep a small stack of newspapers for the purpose of soaking up kitchen spills or for storing breakables during transportation, then automatically toss away any buildup over 3 inches. This is best done by starting at the bottom of the pile so to avoid paper mites.

You might not realize, but expired coupons can be donated to troops serving overseas. The military personnel and their families can use these up to six months past their expiry date. Just search on Google to find out how you can send the coupons and in doing so help a military family who is often only living on one income.

To sum up, once your paper-based clutter has been identified and sorted, it is then time to start addressing the other problem areas. To do this we will use one of the most effective methods known to the experienced de-clutterer.

The Easiest De-cluttering Method

One of the easiest methods to help you reorganize any room or space in your home is what's called The Five Box Method. To do this you are going to need, as the name suggests, five boxes.

Label, each box as follows:

Garbage

Recycle/Sell

Keep

Sentimental

Unsure

When you have the boxes ready, then enter the room in which you wish to start and go through every non-essential item making sure that you have assigned it to a box. Be prepared to be ruthless when deciding on items for the "recycle/sell" and "garbage" boxes because it's these that have inevitably caused much of the clutter in the first place.

When thinking about discarding such items it is important to consider the last time you used it. If the item in question has not been used in over a year, then there is a strong possibility that it's no longer required. If you are still undecided, then use the "unsure" box, but be careful not to overload this category as you will need to address this again in the future.

Following this exercise, the remainder of your items should be fairly easy to sort through because it will just be a case of identifying the 'keep' items from the sentimental stuff. Anything labeled as "keep" will need to go back in the room in an organized manner while all sentimental items will need to be boxed up and stored in an appropriate place. When reviewing the sentimental stuff, it is important to maintain a consistent approach and remain ruthless. Keeping old photos and cherished belongings are perfectly acceptable, but try to avoid keeping unwanted wedding gifts or birthday presents just because you feel guilty about getting rid of them.

Anything labeled as "unsure" should be boxed and sealed up. This box should then be stored in the basement, loft, or garage and reviewed again in six months. The chances are that if the box has remained sealed and not looked at for that time period, then the items inside are no longer required. If that is the case, then discard the contents of the box.

After completing this exercise, you should see a major difference in that particular room. The next stage of the process will be to organize the room more effectively so that every item has a home. In theory, every item should be put in a logical place and preferably with other similar items. Grouping them together will also help you establish how much storage space will be needed and so you will be working more efficiently.

When grouping items it is important to remember the following key points:

– Group related objects and assemble them together

– Throw away unwanted or duplicate items

– Select storage boxes or filing areas for each grouping

– Decide where to store each box and try to store grouped items close to the area they are used

If you would like to consider adopting a slightly more ruthless approach to the Five Box Method, then you could use the Three Box Method.

Essentially the Three Box Method uses the same idea as the Five Box Method, but has no box for "unsure" or "sentimental" items. This is because it helps promote a more streamlined and efficient system that eliminates the option of keeping items that are non-essential.

Now that you have a system to work with you can start to tackle each room individually. For the sake of this we will address the different rooms of a typical house in the following order, but there is no hard or fast rule so this can be adapted to suit your own home.

The Living Room

The living room is one of the most important rooms in the house. It is important to maintain an organized living space as this is an area where people will like to spend their time relaxing. If the room is full of clutter, then it will be difficult to relax. Here are some useful tips to help with the process:

Before you start to de-clutter the room (or for that matter any room in your home) sit in your favorite seat and have a look around the living space. Make a note of the cluttered areas that bother you. You might even try to not focus on the particular items themselves, but try to determine what you want from the room itself. Do the items in the room help to create the vision you want for your room? If the items don't, then they must go, so tackling these first with your five boxes will be one sure method.

Use a rack to store all of the current papers and magazines that you are using. This will stop you from dumping your reading material on the coffee table or on the floor beside the chair or sofa.

Go through all of your DVD's and books; have a clear out and tidy what's left. If there are films or books that you didn't particularly enjoy watching, then consider selling or giving them away. Additionally, if you have a book or DVD in your collection that belonged to a friend, then make a point of returning it. All of the books and DVD's that remain should be sorted in their relevant cabinet or shelf so that everything is facing the same way (title of book/DVD facing you when you look at it).

If you have a lot of books you would like clear, then how about having a book swap? Invite your guests to bring their unwanted books and a bag. Everyone can exchange the books they want and take them home in their bags. Anything left can be donated to a library or charity store.

Find a home for all of the remote controls. Don't just leave them on the arm of the sofa as they will inevitably end up down the back of it or on the floor. Maybe you could keep them in a basket?

Get behind the TV and other electrical items and have a sort out of all the cables. Identify which cable belongs to what piece of equipment and label it. You could even buy some cable-tidy clips that allow you to fasten the cables together and give a better look.

The Kitchen

"The more you dislike doing something, the more often you should do it."

De-cluttering the kitchen can be a daunting task. At first glance it may appear organized, but after opening all the cupboards and drawers you may soon notice that there is no logic to your current methods and much of what is being stored has very little use.

Before starting, make sure your kitchen has been cleaned to its usual state of cleanliness. Empty the dishwasher and make sure all the counters are clear. Then fill the sink with hot soapy water so any dusty items can be quickly cleaned. Also, ensure you have a good supply of garbage bags available - you're probably going to need them!

Do each part of your kitchen step-by-step. De-clutter a single draw or cupboard one at a time and don't try to rush things. Have a break if needs be or make sure the kids are okay in the other room. You could even deep clean each area as you go along, but just make sure you keep everything manageable.

Show no mercy when you are clearing out the cupboards. Empty out everything first and see what you need and what you don't. If you have saucepans or baking equipment that have not been used for some time, then it's time to let them go. Ask yourself how often you have used that pasta-making machine. If it was only once two years ago, then it has to go. Don't start saying to yourself, "But this cost me so-and-so many dollars" or "One day this will be worth something." If you don't use it, chuck it!

The only exception is holiday cooking tools such as twelve-day cookie cutters or chocolate Easter-bunny molds. These can be kept elsewhere in the home, such as with the Christmas decorations. This will ensure you free up valuable active space in the kitchen.

When you get to the utensils draw, remove everything and wipe the draw clean. Only the utensils you know you will use should be returned to the draw.

Clear out any out-of-date foodstuffs from cupboards and pantries. Ask yourself whether you need three jars of oregano in your spice collection. Empty out the fridge, get right to the back of it and clean.

Don't forget your junk draw. I'm sure you have one. That's the one where you keep scissors, pens, sticky tape, a pocket screwdriver, and that broken-off handle from your favorite coffee mug which you still haven't got around to gluing back on. You never know, you might be surprised what you might find in there, and anyway, it's going to need cleaning out because I'm sure you will soon have even more junk to put back in.

As you go along don't get side tracked. Don't go looking for that recipe for chocolate cake after finding that old packet of chocolate buttons on the top shelf of the cupboard. Just keep focused on the job at hand.

When you are left with the items that you wish to keep, you should consider splitting them into three groups:

1. Items that are regularly used

2. Items that are occasionally used

3. Items that are never used

Review the last group again and consider the last time you actually used the item. Get rid of it, if you can, or adopt the method of using the "unsure box". Store it somewhere and review the box in a few months. If you have still had no use for it in that time, then it's no longer needed.

Also give plenty of thought to reorganizing your existing kitchen items. Try to maintain a rule of keeping the items that you use regularly in accessible places and the remainder in areas that are harder to reach. Cooking utensils such as serving spoons, ladles, and whisks should be stored close to the oven, while mugs and glasses should be in close proximity to the kettle and sink. By doing this you will be spending your time in the kitchen more efficiently.

The Dining Room

"Because it's flat, it doesn't mean it's a storage area"

A dining room would be a very simple room to reorganize if its only purpose was for eating meals, but this often isn't the case. Depending on its location in your home, it can in many ways attract more clutter than any other area in the house and the biggest reason for this can be the dining room table. This is because it is very easy for the table to become a 'clutter magnet' for mail, free newspapers, toys, keys, or any other odds and ends that people might bring in. This is often exasperated when one member of the household leaves something on it and the others, after seeing this, think nothing wrong in doing the same. The next thing you know you will have a table buried under a mountain of junk.

As well as being unsightly, some items such as keys when tossed onto the table can actually scratch its surface. You definitely don't want that, so it's time to reclaim the table!

Firstly, avoid leaving mail and newspapers on it. As we had already discussed in an earlier chapter, designate a place at their point of entry into the home, then sort through them, keeping or junking whatever you need and don't need.

Next, make sure you have plenty of hooks by your main entrance for hanging coats, hats, and school bags. The dining room table is not the place to store these items.

Keep a good-sized trashcan near to the table. If it looks unsightly, try to keep it hidden inside a side-table or closet.

One idea is to keep the table pre-set for meals. This would act as a deterrent for anyone who enters and wants to dump their 'stuff' on it.

Finally, whoever is leaving their clutter on the table could be forced to clean it off by themselves before mealtime. Hopefully, this would help them to learn that this is not the area for their clutter.

If the only purpose of dining room is for eating meals, then try to keep items that only fit into this category within the room. This would include items such as crockery, glassware, and cutlery.

Think about the last dinner party that you hosted and what items were used when doing that. If there were any additional bits and pieces that you think you may have used, then also consider finding a home for these within the dining room.

If, on the other hand, your dining room has more than one purpose, then allocate specific storage areas for each one so that clearing up can be completed in a quick and organized manner.

Consider buying a dresser unit or sideboard that can assist with any storage problems. If your dining room is used for many different purposes, then you may need to use the sideboard for storing additional items such as crayons, pens and pencils, or power cords.

Maybe you already have a sideboard that displays your expensive china collection. You may need to ask yourself how often you use this china and whether it would be better stored in a more out-of-the-way area such as on a high shelf. This would free up the sideboard to meet the needs of the space.

If you are also considering buying a new dining room table, then consider one that is round. This would enable you to enjoy the extra space and movement around the table. A round table will also give the room a feeling of being larger.

If your dining room is in constant use, then another option when buying a new table is to go for a sturdy 'pub-style' one. The reason for this is so you can encourage all the members of your household to use it as much as possible and in doing so it will become more difficult for clutter to accumulate. The table can now become the center of family activities, such as playing board games and other fun pursuits.

Something else to consider is maybe buying some fold-out chairs. These can be folded away in a cupboard or pantry and brought out and placed around the table when extra seating is required. We must not forget that it is around the table that friends understand best the warmth of being together.

The Bedrooms

"Bad habits are like a comfortable bed, easy to get into, but hard to get out of"

De-cluttering a bedroom can be notoriously tricky due to the amount of clothing involved and the problem may be exacerbated when you share it with a partner. If this is the case, then it's best to get them involved in the de-cluttering process as well. If not, organizing their clothing may be difficult and could result in disagreements, especially if you start disposing of your partner's favorite garments. The last thing you want now is to have a row.

Before you start to reorganize the bedroom, remove anything that doesn't belong in there. Empty cups, borrowed clothes, and towels should all be returned to their rightful home and any dirty washing placed in the laundry basket.

Use a bin temporarily to throw in any items of clothes which have been left lying around. These can then be returned to their proper home once the bedroom has been cleared.

Remove all clothing from dresser draws and decide if anything should be thrown away. Once that done, fold your clothes and return them back to the drawers while ensuring they are stored logically with similar items together. Keep underwear and socks in drawers that remain accessible.

Try using a slightly modified version of the Five Box Method when dealing with clothes. A simple 3-box technique works better as it tends to make you more ruthless. Have one box for the items you want to keep, another for anything you want to sell or donate, and the third for items that you want to throw away.

Throw away any clothes which are stained, missing buttons, torn, or don't fit. Out-of-season clothes can be stored in the less accessible places such as under the bed. I will talk more about under-the-bed storage later in this book.

If you still find that you have too many clothes in your closet, then consider using a technique called the "Hanger Trick". You can either start by turning all the items in your closet so that the coat hangers are facing the wrong way or place sticky labels on each hanger. When you wear a particular item, you should turn the hanger round or remove the label. Over the course of the next few months, you will gradually see a pattern forming and will probably be surprised as to what gets used and what doesn't. Review the situation after a few months and remove items that you no longer wear.

Don't get into the habit of leaving clothes on the bed, but always return them straight to their designated place. Also, get into the habit of making your bed every day if it is something you don't do already.

Now organize any bedside tables. Make sure any items such as coffee mugs or books are returned to their correct home and lotions and nail files have been placed back in the bathroom.

If you do have some sentimental items you would like to keep but don't want to display, then store them in a "memory box".

Apply a little thought to available storage areas in the bedroom. If space is at a premium, then consider stacking storage containers in the closet and putting up shelves to provide extra storage room.

If you have a mini-office in your bedroom, then consider finding a new location for it because the last thing you want to be thinking about as your drift off to sleep are those unanswered emails. Anywhere else in the home would be a preferable but, obviously, this depends on the space you have available.

When reorganizing a kid's room it may require a little more planning as toys and games will come into the equation. Try sorting these items into groups and then storing them together in labeled boxes. An example of this would be to have books in one box and all dolls/action figures in another. It's important to accept that at some point in the future you will probably walk into their room and see everything scattered across the floor. When this happens, it will be a far less painful process to clear it away knowing that there are boxes available to hold everything.

Establishing a home for all of your kids' toys and games will also assist with getting them to understand the concept of clearing up. Hopefully, with a little encouragement, this will lead to them doing it by themselves.

The Bathroom

"Reality is only seen when the mirror is clean"

Organizing a bathroom can sometimes be tricky because it is often one of the smallest rooms in the house yet is one regularly used. Because of this, it can be brimming with toiletries, shower supplies, cleaning supplies, makeup, and all sorts of oddities, so having a targeted and ruthless de-cluttering method is going to be essential. For this reason, we are going to use a 3-box method.

This 3-Box method will consist of one box for items that need to be returned to their correct place in the bathroom, another box for items which are used less and could be stored away, and the third is for items we can sale or donate. Finally, we will need a plastic garbage bag for anything that is going to be trashed.

To start reorganizing your bathroom it is best to begin by going through all of the toiletries, cleaning supplies and medicines and discard anything that is empty, old, or unused.

When reviewing makeup and perfumes it is worth remembering that mascara should be replaced every few months and that perfumes tend to last three to four years before they expire.

Consider how many towels you need in your bathroom. Could some of these be stored elsewhere? Better still, how many towels does your family really need? Maybe you have too many so some could be given away or trashed. The same goes for multiples of shaving brushes or your favorite hand soap. Don't hold onto anything by self-talking yourself into saying "just in case" because it has to go – now!

Don't forget to look in the shower. Are there any toys that can be returned to their correct place in the kid's room? Is it jam-packed with half-used bottles? If it is and you have two half-full bottles containing something similar such as shampoo, you could pour the contents of one into the other and then throw away the empty bottle.

As you remove these items give the area a good clean. It might have been a long time since some of these surfaces have seen the light of day and who knows what type of grime might have started to buildup there.

If the same items continually appear where they shouldn't, such as a brush in a drawer or a piece of jewelry, then maybe you should consider making this their new home because it seems they are better off there than where they should be.

Think about the most suitable storage options for your bathroom. Small cabinets, shelves, and wicker baskets will all add much needed storage space if you need it.

Also, consider where each item should be stored. If it is used on a daily basis, such as a toothbrush or razor, then it should be stored somewhere which is accessible. Try to avoid cluttering up these areas when placing these items.

In areas that are not so easy to reach, you should store items that are used less frequently. These could be the things used on a weekly or monthly basis.

As you return these items, give them a good wipe with a damp cloth as they could have become as dirty as the surface they were standing on.

Shampoo and shower gel can be placed in a shower-caddy and hung off the showerhead, so preventing them from cluttering up the floor.

Consider fixing towel rails to the walls and place hooks on the back of the bathroom door. This frees up more space and gives a home to the dressing gowns, towels, and other garments.

Once you have finished de-cluttering the bathroom, the last thing you need to do is to relax in a hot bathtub and congratulate yourself on a job well done.

The Home Office

To be successful in business you need to be organized and competent and so the last thing you want to be doing is to work in a room cluttered with mess. Have a think about your own home office. Are there piles of papers or boxes and files blocking the walkways? Have books been carelessly strewn about? Maybe that box of Christmas decorations which you've been meaning to put up into the loft is still blocking the front of the filing cabinet. If this is the case, then consider what visiting clients would think should they see this state of disorganization? What would it tell them about your effectiveness and natural talent? Hmmm, I'll let you guess that one.

Now you are probably telling yourself that the reason for all this clutter is that you don't want to take time-out from your busy work schedule to keep it tidy. But let's just think for a minute. What effect will all this clutter be having on your own work performance? Are you missing or even forgetting deadlines because of a misplaced item? Are you wasting valuable time foraging through the clutter for that important document? We've all been there and know how it can negatively affect our productivity.

Scientists have actually found that due to physical clutter we are unable to focus and process information effectively. This will result in procrastination rearing its ugly head again, so let's get back on track and reclaim your office so you can devote your time to business – not endlessly wading through clutter. Remember this: organization is the cornerstone of any successful business.

Where to start?

To begin with, do a quick scan and see what doesn't belong in your office. Are there coffee mugs that need returning to the kitchen and is that box of Christmas decorations still waiting to be moved into the loft?

To help with your de-cluttering, you can once again use the trusty box method. You will need one box for things you want to keep, one for things that live elsewhere in the home, and one for donations. You will also need a forth box or a garbage bag for anything which needs to be trashed.

Let's take a look at the walkways first. Clear away any obstructions so the entrance, desk, and documents cabinets are easily accessible. This is important because we want to ensure that we can remove the remaining clutter safely and without hindrance.

Now look at your desk and how it fits into the room. Is it the right size? If it's too big, it could be taking up unnecessary space, whereas a desk which is too small could have its workspace increased by placing a small table next to it.

How about the other furniture in the room? Giving each piece of office equipment its own piece of furniture would help with extra storage. An example would be a small cabinet to hold a printer could also house in its draw replacement ink cartridges and paper.

On the subject of office equipment, if you have one of those old fax machines, ask yourself whether you really need it. You could replace it with an all-in-one printer/scanner/copier/fax. These all-round machines have come down a lot in price and can now be bought quite cheaply.

Books and files should be kept on a bookshelf that could be either freestanding or fitted. These files could be arranged as both current and archive and as well as being kept in alphabetical order. Make sure your desk is positioned so you can easily reach these areas from your chair. The same goes for any document cabinet. Preferably, have it situated behind your chair so you can limit the amount of times you'll need to get up and down.

Let's now take a look at the desk in more detail.

I expect paper is the main culprit for clutter on your desk. To overcome this, consider using a step file or having a stack of trays. You could label these trays "inbox" and "outbox". Make sure all paperwork is labeled clearly.

Think carefully whether paperwork needs to be kept or not and decide if printing something is really necessary. If you do want to keep paperwork, maybe it could be scanned and saved digitally on your computer.

For the drawers, consider visiting an office supply store and purchasing some draw organizers. These can be plastic trays and caddies and will be perfect for holding any pens, paperclips, etc.

If you are in need of a new desk, consider buying what's called a Geek Desk. Many users have recommended these as being the best and most versatile type for any home office and it's not hard to see why. These innovative desks are fully adjustable and can be raised or lowered. There's even an area at the back for hiding unsightly electrical cables.

On the subject of electrical cables, let's take a look at your own. These can often be the cause of clutter behind the desk, which then have the knock-on-effect of causing high levels of dust to buildup. This can be alleviated by using some cable tidy clips that are great for returning order to an area of entanglement.

To keep on top of things, consider purging the clutter from your office regularly. Decide which category below each item falls into:

Act on it

Throw it

File it

Purging regularly would only involve a short amount of time and the result would be a nice relaxed and controlled environment for doing your business. Wouldn't you like that?

The Utility/Wash Room

Before you start to reorganize your utility room, it's important to establish what purpose it will serve in your home. It may be a room that you want to dedicate to just laundry and ironing, while on the other hand it might be used as an extension to the garage with the space being utilized for storage.

To begin with, try listing all of the items that you want to store in the utility room and then allocate a shelf, cupboard, or other suitable storage area for them. If it does not belong there, then throw it out.

Avoid storing cleaning products and other hazardous items in areas that can be reached by young children. Instead, consider using high-level shelving or storage units for such items.

If your utility room is used for laundry purposes, then try to maintain a regular routine that allows you to stay on top of dirty washing. Performing laundry duties every few days will help to avoid a buildup.

If you have the space, consider purchasing a three-bin hamper or separate hampers. These can be used for storing whites, colors, and items that need to be washed by hand.

A vertical shelf unit can maximize your storage options and a collection of containers such as boxes or baskets are excellent for holding clothespins, brushes, or scissors. Another spare container can also be used as the central point for holding items found in the pockets of clothes. That means everyone in the home will then know where to go when they are looking for these items.

Remember this: doing the laundry can be "loads of fun".

Under the Stairs

The storage space under the stairs can often be one of the worst places for clutter because it can become a bit of a dumping ground for everything and anything.

Before you start the process of de-cluttering this area, you will need to think about what you want to store there. You may want it as an area to keep your coats or it could be the new shoe cupboard, but whatever you decide, it's important to have the idea in place before you start.

With your plan in mind, first pull out everything from inside and give the area a good clean. Before returning the items back to their rightful place, give them a good sort through because you might be surprised what you could find. Once again, be ruthless about discarding anything that is unused or broken.

If coats are going in there, then consider investing in a coat rack. Similarly, if it is shoes, then buy a good-sized shoe rack. Also, consider storing bulky items like the vacuum cleaner and ironing board if they don't have a home anywhere else.

Should you decide that you want to use it as a general storage area, then consider the idea of buying or building a storage unit. Be creative when thinking about this and consider what you would want to house in there. If finances allow, then consider getting a professional to design and build it because this can really utilize all the available space and transform it into a new feature within your home.

The Garage

A garage can be a useful area for storage and these days many garages are used to store more than just the car. In fact, a UCLA study found that 75 percent of people did not use their garage for the car, but instead used it for "stuff". Baring that in mind, when de-cluttering your home it is important to avoid dumping your excess belongings into the garage just because you can't find a place for them in the house.

Primarily, garages should be used to store bulky items like tools, bikes, barbeques, lawnmowers, and other such items that are not considered suitable for the house. However, what happens when your garage has been a "dumping ground" for all your clutter and the time has come for a major purge? The prospect could be quite daunting, but don't worry because there is an easy way for tackling this.

Firstly, you don't want to try to attempt to do it all in one go. Instead, break it down into manageable chunks. For example, maybe you have only one hour free today. You could then just spend that hour sorting through boxes. You could move onto the next task once you have some more free time. As you do so, keep repeating to yourself, "slow and steady, slow and steady, slow and steady," and as you complete each task, you will feel the momentum building. Before you know it, you will have a clean clutter-free garage.

If you have chosen a sunny day for de-cluttering then you could remove the items and lay them out on the driveway. This will make it easier to sort through and to decide what needs to stay and what can go. You may need to have a vehicle on standby that will be able to carry your unwanted, larger items to either a charity store or the local dump.

If you have items that have not been used in over a year or so, then consider discarding them. Think about the best ways of the storing the ones you want to keep but only use occasionally. Plastic storage bins are an excellent option and they can be very inexpensive to purchase. These can come in a number of sizes with the smaller ones being stored on shelves.

Think vertically because garage walls often have plenty of space to utilize. Use heavy duty hooks on the garage walls to hang your power and garden tools. You could also consider using these or racks to hang bicycles. Using strong shelving will create extra space and avoid storing items on the floor.

Don't forget the ceiling, too. Special ceiling hooks can be purchased from hardware stores for hanging everything from bikes to ladders. One thing you want to avoid is having walkways blocked by bikes.

If sporting equipment is often left in a pile in one corner of the garage, then consider getting a freestanding sports organizer. These will hold everything from baseball bats to soccer balls and will definitely help bring order to where chaos usually reigns. These sports organizers, or sports racks as they're also known, can be purchased in good hardware stores or online.

Try to store items regularly used near to the front of the garage or otherwise keep them in an easily accessible area.

Now that your garage is once again looking clean and orderly and the car is able to fit back in, simply ask yourself this:

'Doesn't that feel good?'

How to De-clutter a Small Apartment

To de-clutter your apartment you will need to use the same methods and principals as you would for any other home, but with a little more ruthlessness and organization. This is because apartments tend to lack space and have even less storage areas.

Like before, it's best to make a plan of how you want the room to look after the transition. To do this, review each room to see what areas need reorganization, and what storage solutions are available. Once you have done that, you can then approach the task on a room-by-room basis, ensuring that you don't try to do any more than this at a time.

Deal with paperwork in the same way we have discussed earlier. You will also need to use the Five Box or Three Box Methods when sorting through the clutter. Because you need to be a little more ruthless when living in an apartment, I would personally suggest adopting the Three Box Method.

It is often said that, we use 20 percent of our stuff, 80 percent of the time, so when thinking about individual items consider the purpose of it and the last time it was used. If it's over 12 months since the item was last used, then seriously consider throwing it away. Getting rid of things can actually be very liberating.

One of the key areas of reorganizing an apartment is too utilize storage and maintain an organized lifestyle in the future. Consider investing in furniture that has more than one purpose. For example, a sofa bed could be used for seating in a lounge and opened out as a bed for guests in the evening. With this in mind, you may be tempted to transform your second bedroom into a study by simply getting rid of that hardly-used bed, and replacing it with additional storage units.

Under-bed storage and closet organizers can provide additional storage space in the bedroom, and if you are thinking about buying under-bed storage, then look for ones with wheels attached. These will make life a lot easier in the "long run".

Closet organizers come in many different forms, so try a little research before purchasing. Alternatively, consider giving your closet a new look by building some shelves inside or installing additional hanging rails.

The key to living clutter-free in an apartment is to think vertically, so consider what items can be hung on the wall. These can range from the obvious, such as bookshelves, to the less obvious, such as bicycle-racks. You could even consider using the space over the doors for fitting extra shelving.

To continue maintaining an uncluttered apartment requires dealing with clutter as and when it arises. Be strict when you go shopping by saying to yourself "Nothing can come in, unless an equal amount goes out." Also, try to avoid putting off household chores by creating a routine of clearing away mess each day before you go to bed. Keeping on top of it is paramount because your goal should be a spacious and comfortable apartment where you can relax and be content.

How to Remove Anxiety and Stop Feeling Guilty When You've Thrown Your Things Away

Many of us will struggle with disposing of unwanted items because we often get an overwhelming sense of guilt. This can be from throwing away gifts that other people have given us or because of the amount of money we had originally spent on them. In either case it's never a good idea to dwell on the situation. If you are dealing with an unwanted gift, then think about the last time you used it and whether you would actually want to again. Try to avoid thinking about the person that gave it to you. In addition, try to avoid thinking about the original cost of things you are throwing away. Dwelling on these matters will not help and will only cause unnecessary anxiety. Only focus on the positive aspects of removing it from your home. Your home will look better and, potentially, it could be given to someone who would actually use it.

Another issue to be aware of when disposing of unwanted things is emotional attachment. Whilst it is perfectly acceptable to want to keep photos and memorabilia that relate to your past or a deceased relative, it is also important to realize that discarding such items is not disrespectful or damaging to the memories of past events. Try to limit the number of sentimental items you keep and only choose the smaller ones that can be stored away in a memory box.

Dealing with feelings of guilt and anxiety are perfectly normal when de-cluttering your home, but these feelings should not stop you from completing the task. Once you have decided that an item is not worth keeping, it should be disposed of in the most suitable way and then forgotten about.

Sometimes you may decide that you no longer want an item, but the monetary value attached may tempt you into reselling it. If this is the case, successfully recouping some of its original cost might help you to overcome any guilt or anxiety. This money can then be spent on something you really need.

If you are really undecided about a particular item then consider using the "unsure" box and review the situation again in a few months.

How Many Clothes and Toys Do We All Really Need?

Clothing and toys are often the main sources of clutter in the home. A change in season or fashions usually results in the addition of new clothing to the wardrobe, while older and rarely worn items are seldom removed. This results in our closets quickly becoming overstocked.

So how do we stop this? Simple! For every new piece of clothing you add, select an older/unused item to remove. You are effectively adopting a 'one in, one out' approach to the situation.

The same problem occurs with toys. As kids grow older they will inevitably receive them for their birthday and at Christmas, but this doesn't always result in the parents having a clear-out of the older items, many of which probably haven't been played with for some time. Another thing to consider is that, as children get older, often their toys get bigger - so the clutter gets bigger too.

To combat this, the 'one in, one out' method can be applied to toys in the same way as it was to clothing. Just be prepared that you may have difficulty getting the child to give up one of their toys if they think they are going to lose it. You may suddenly find they have gained a new found love for it. To avoid this, to try removing the toy without the child's knowledge. This can either be done when they are asleep or not around.

Alternatively, you could try rotating the toys to help overcome the problem. This method involves selecting some and storing them away in the loft or cupboard for a short time. After a few weeks reintroduce the toys that have been stored away and select some new ones to replace them in storage. This strategy makes the child appreciate the toys more while reducing the number on show and hence the clutter they make.

One great way to de-clutter toys is to temporarily hide the ones they don't play with in a storage box somewhere out of sight. If they ask for the toy, give it back to them, but if after a while they never mention it, then you know it can be safely donated or thrown away.

How to Teach Your Kids to De-clutter

Teaching your kids to de-clutter is never going to be an easy task because for many this will be their first experience of loss. To overcome this, you must try to make the whole de-cluttering experience as fun as possible.

One solution is to make it into a kind of game. Give each of your kids a small basket and an allotted time – 10 minutes is always good because they won't begin to get bored - and they have to race around and throw away as much as they can. They should also return items which they want to keep to their correct places.

Rewards can be given to the kid who has collected the most or for the first to clear a designated area. You could also liven things up by playing music and dancing - in fact the whole family can join in! I'm sure you may have at least one 'grown-up' kid in your home, too!

If there are any items, your child is unsure about parting with, then explain that you are going to be place them in the "unsure box". If at any time over the following week they want the item back, they can then remove it from the box. If at the end of the week the item is still there, then dispose of it. Depending on your child, you could rationally point out the reasons why the item is being disposed of. In other cases, it might be better to just do it secretly.

Disposable items can be donated to charity and this can be explained to your child, preferably before they begin the de-cluttering process. This would help them to understand the purpose of what they are doing and the worth the items might have to a child, less fortunate than they are. Maybe your child could even help you to choose which charity to donate to.

Once the de-cluttering process is complete, you could take your child to the charity with you to drop off their toys. This would help them to gain a full sense of value of what they are doing and how their actions are helping those in need.

For broken items, or those missing a part, set a rule that they must be thrown away. This will help your kids to care more about their toys. You could also teach your kids to put one item away before getting another out and so cutting down on mess.

For artwork, have an area where it can be displayed on rotation. Explain to your kids that when a new piece has been painted, an old one must go.

Finally, you must respect your kids' feelings and take a gentle approach when introducing these lifestyle changes. However, these will teach your kids to respect themselves, their possessions, and the people around them – some of the most important lessons they can learn in life.

How to Convince Someone Who Is a Hoarder to De-clutter Their Home

A hoarder is an individual that accumulates belongings of little or no value and shows an unwillingness to dispose of them. This type of behavior can be a major contributing factor to a cluttered home. Obsessive hoarding is actually classed as a medical condition that can cause serious problems if not dealt with properly.

Severe cases of hoarding can be classified as a health and safety risk as it increases the chances of fire due to the abnormally high amount of flammable objects kept in the home. It can also create problems, when trying to escape a fire, because corridors and doorways will be blocked. In the most severe cases, the weight of these objects can also cause structural damage to the property if stored inappropriately.

Most people that suffer from a hoarding problem tend to accumulate possessions for the same reasons as anyone else. Either they become emotionally attached to an item, so develop a fear of letting it go or they think the item will prove useful in the future and so are concerned that they will need it after throwing it away.

Hoarding can be broken down into three parts. Firstly, an object is obtained. Next, there will be a reluctance to dispose of it when the item is no longer needed. Finally, there will be a lack of organization regarding this, leading to clutter.

Trying to convince a hoarder to de-clutter is no easy task, but when doing so, it is important to highlight the benefits of having an organized home. Make them aware of the time they will save when looking for things in the future. Tell them about the good that will be achieved when they recycle their unwanted items and mention the risks that are associated with hoarding. Hopefully this will kick-start them into doing something.

When dealing with problems of this nature, it is important that the person involved is made aware of the amount of time and effort that will be required for reorganizing the home. It is also essential that they understand that this will be ongoing in order to avoid the buildup of clutter in the future.

If the person seems overwhelmed by the amount of clutter, then encourage them to take small steps towards completing the project. Start by spending five minutes on the task and then gradually buildup the time spent reorganizing. Set personal targets for getting areas clear within a certain timeframe and encourage the person to include the de-cluttering task in their daily routine. My 10-minute (or less) plan later in this book could help them to see that this can in fact be very manageable.

Sometimes the offer of help may be appreciated, as it will lighten the workload for the person involved. Providing them with a second opinion (as in a 'clutter buddy') can also help when decisions need to be made on throwing things away. It's unlikely that the person helping will hold any sentiment towards the items causing the clutter and so they will be able to offer a more impartial opinion.

The Best Websites for Getting Rid of Your Home Clutter

Selling your unwanted items can be a great way to clear clutter and can, in some cases, be quite lucrative as well. There are many different websites that can be used to sell your unwanted items, with the most popular and well-known being eBay. This site allows most things to be sold and it's very easy to begin the process. You will be required to register and create an account with them and it's probably best to create a PayPal account to assist with receiving any potential funds from the sale.

Other less well-known sites can also be a used to sell your clutter. What follows is a list of these, along with information for each:

Gazelle.com – good for selling electronic items such as cell phones, cameras and laptops.

NextWorth.com – offers gift cards in exchange for old electronic items.

TuneCycle.com – pays cash for old iPods and computers that are broken.

ReCellular.com – will buy your old cell phones.

Cash4Books.net – buys books and will even pay for shipping in most cases.

Borders – a well-known bookstore that offers cash for books.

PaperBackSwap.com – send your books to them and they will give you credits. Then use these credits to buy other books from them.

PlatosCloset.com – buys clothing and specializes in teen/young adults fashions.

ThredUp.com – more of a swap store for younger children and allows toys to be exchanged.

WhatSellsBest.com – more of a review site that helps to gain a rough idea on price.

Etsy.com – useful for selling more unique items such as antiques.

DiggersList.com – bit like eBay in that it sells most things.

Freecycle.com – not a selling site but useful if you are just looking to give something away to a good home.

Craigslist.com – A huge free-listing site for almost anything.

How to Get a Tax Refund for Your Charity Donations

If you didn't know already, donating your clutter to a charity could make you eligible for a tax deduction, so let's find out exactly how.

Before starting, ensure that the charitable organization you are interested in giving to qualifies you to make tax deductible donations. You will find most will, but there are some that won't, so check first. To find out, simply ask and they will be able to tell you, otherwise, you can check on the IRS website to see if they are listed.

The next step is to ensure that the items are in "good condition or better". This is a requirement by the IRS. Avoid donating items such as socks and underwear, unless they are "like new". Could you imagine walking around in someone else's used panties!

Make a spreadsheet of the items you are donating and include their purchase price, their approximate date of purchase, their condition, and their donation date. To work out the value of your items you will need to estimate their fair market value. For those of you who don't know what 'fair market value' means, this is how much you would offer the item for sale on Ebay and how much a buyer would expect to pay. To help with this, www.goodwill.org publishes on their website the fair market value guidelines for many common items. Don't be surprised if your expensive sweater is valued lower than you expected. This is because it will be quoted at the same fair-market value as one bought in a discount store.

Never overestimate the value of items because many people have previously tried to abuse the system in this way. For high value items, such as furniture, and electronic products like computers, take photographs of each.

If you donate an item or a group of items that exceed $5,000 in value, you may need to have a qualified appraisal. They will fill in the information for Part III, "Declaration of Appraiser" in Section B of the IRS Form 8283.

Don't just throw everything into a large bag when you take it to the charity. You want to ensure everything is in order so you will be able to have accurate documentation. You should always provide the IRS with the correct documentation or you could find yourself liable for a tax audit.

When the charity receives your donation, they will give you a receipt in order to claim the deduction. You must also file your tax return with IRS Form 1040 and itemize the deductions in Schedule A. If the items come to a total value of more than $500, then you must also file Form 8283 with your return.

Your tax will be deductible only in the same year as when you made the donation, so make sure your donation is made before December 31 of the year you want to claim for.

Because everyone's circumstances can be quite different, you should contact a certified CPA or accountant if you have any detailed questions.

The 10-Minutes (or Less) Clutter-Free Action Plan

Once you've finished de-cluttering your home, it will then be important to keep on top of any future buildup. The last thing you want to see are the results of all your hard work slowly disappearing as it returns to how it was before. To achieve this you'll need to follow some kind of plan and in this chapter I have one which should do just that.

Each part of my action plan only takes 10 minutes to do and in some cases even less. You can mix and match the different parts together depending on how much time is available and these can be easily adapted to the needs for your own home. One thing is certain; it will definitely stop you from becoming overwhelmed by any future clutter.

Before we begin, let's take a look at 'time', and I'm talking about *your* time. Ten minutes can actually be quite long, so think about the instances when you might have this available. Here are some suggestions:

- While waiting for the kettle to boil and your tea to brew

- During the commercial break when you are watching a show

- Between the steps of preparing your dinner

- While you are waiting for a friend to arrive

Now let's take a look at each part of the 10-minute plan:

Part 1: Living Room.

1) Sit down and survey the room. Do you see any distracting piles? If so, then de-clutter.

2) Tidy away or dispose of Magazines and newspapers.

3) Rearrange the cushions on the sofa and chairs.

4) Gather up remote controls and return to where they belong.

5) Rearrange any books on the bookshelf if they are facing the wrong way.

Part 2: Kitchen

1) Load or empty the dishwasher.

2) Return any items around the sink to their rightful place.

3) Straighten your spice collection so labels are facing the right way.

4) Pick up bottles that have fallen over, and return any misplaced ones to where they belong.

5) Remove anything from the fridge that is old or rotten.

6) Collect up any plastic bags and store in a central location for re-use.

7) Tidy your utensils and organize any that have been misplaced.

8) Organize your Tupperware and Pyrex collections as you did with the utensils.

9) Organize any coupons.

10) Organize your cookbooks.

11) Organize take-out menus and dispose of any you don't want.

12) Purge your pantry of anything you don't have a use for.

Part 3: Dining Room

1) Remove any items from the dining room table and return them to their correct place.

2) Ensure the sideboards are clear and everything in the drawers and cabinets is where it belongs.

Part 4: Bedrooms

1) Choose one draw in your dresser and remove everything. Then refold the items and stack.

2) Tidy your night table and remove anything that doesn't belong there.

Part 5: Closet

1) Sort out your hanging clothes and organize. Move the most worn items to an easily accessible location.

2) Match and pair your socks.

3) Organize any shoes and return to their rightful place.

Part 6: Bathroom

1) Take an inventory of bathroom supplies. Check the dates on items to see whether any have expired (Note: This could be done while you are cleaning your teeth).

2) Remove any items from the bathroom that don't belong there and return them to their rightful place.

Part 7: Home Office

1) Go through one file draw and de-clutter.

2) File receipts.

3) Add any notes containing contact details to your contacts list.

4) Add any notes containing appointments to your calendar or diary.

5) De-clutter your desktop and arrange items orderly.

6) De-clutter one desk drawer.

Part 8: Entranceway

1) De-clutter any paperwork, such as mail, leaflets, invitations, or expired coupons.

2) Gather up any shoes or umbrellas and return them to their rightful place.

3) De-clutter your handbag and purse.

Part 9: Garage

1) Choose one collection of tools, sports equipment, or cleaning products and de-clutter. Dispose of anything that isn't needed.

One great idea to keep you focused when you have a spare 20 minutes or so is to set a kitchen timer and then race to complete two parts within the time. This can also be a great motivator when having to do the more unpleasant household chores because you can see how many can be completed before the alarm goes off.

Let's now end this chapter with a great saying you should remember when deciding what items to throw into the recycle bin:

> "One thing you can't recycle is wasted time."

The Best Space-Saving Tips

The best way to approach the subject of saving space is to try and think creatively about the way you use an area and the type of storage you can use it for. You would be surprised by the solutions you could find, using a just a little imagination.

If your home has plenty of bare wall space, then once again 'think vertically'. Use shelving in conjunction with small boxes to store smaller items that may clutter the floor. Also, consider making the use of available space by adding additional shelving to your existing kitchen cabinets or bedroom closet. If you have many photos on show, then consider hanging them on the walls to minimize the clutter on mantelpieces and side units.

Multipurpose furniture is another useful way to save space. Consider buying a coffee table that has built-in storage areas or use an ottoman-style unit instead. Many different styles of ottomans are available on the market and selecting a low-level one with a flat lid will give you the option of using it as a table whilst also offering plenty of storage inside. In addition, other units are available that can double-up as a seated area.

Books and DVD's can be a constant source of clutter, but this problem can be easily resolved by using bookcases or similar storage units. Corner bookcases can be used to fill an empty corner space and low-level storage units can be used to fill an area under a window.

If space is very limited, then think about changing the style of interior door. Bi-folding types can be a good alternative to the traditional door because they need less space to open and close in. Sliding doors also only use the space alongside the wall they are attached to. Items associated with a room, can be hung from hooks on the doors. Hooks attached to a bathroom door may be used to hang towels while ones on a bedroom door could hold dressing gowns or jackets.

The subject of home storage is huge and cannot be covered fully in a single chapter, but if you would like to know more, my book, 'Out of Sight, Out of Mind - Easy Home Organization Tips and Storage Solutions for Clutter-Free Living', is devoted entirely to the subject and includes an in-depth look at each room in the home and more.

Some of the novel ideas found inside its pages will really get you thinking 'out of the box' …or should I say 'out of the storage box'.

In the meantime, we are going to concentrate on two key storage areas and see how we can fully utilize them.

First up, is under the bed.

Making Use of the Storage Area under Your Bed

Another useful space saving tip for the bedroom is to use under-bed storage. If the space under your bed is empty, then consider buying flat storage containers that fit underneath. Some of these even come with wheels to assist with pulling them in and out easily.

When selecting your under-bed storage, be sure to have the measurements of the bed with you. It is important to make the most of the space available, so measure the width of the bed and the height between the floor and the bottom before purchasing.

If you want to exploit this space to its maximum, try raising the bed with supports. Risers are widely available, as well as being fairly cheap, and will allow you to raise the height of the bed from three to eight inches depending on the type you buy. They are very easy to fit and no tools are needed.

If you have a teenager with a small bedroom, you could even raise their bed onto a couple of low-level bookshelves. Space these evenly apart width-way along the length of the bed. This will provide a huge amount of storage where items can be kept underneath in an organized manner.

If you want to be really adventurous, you could build a loft-bed in your teenager's room. The ones I've seen have either been built from wood or scaffolding poles. These are great because they leave the whole space beneath them for living in and provide a fun climb up to bed every night.

Do Those Space Bags Really Work?

Space-bags are a relatively new idea and generally seem to have received positive feedback from users. They become very compact by sucking out all the air from the bags so they contract around the items inside. To use, fill the bag with your items, then seal it using the inbuilt zip-lock. Once sealed, simply attach your vacuum hose to the valve and extract all the air from the bag. Some manufacturers claim these can triple your storage space whilst providing better protection against water damage, mildew, dirt, and bugs.

Space bags will create space with minimal effort and they work best when storing clothing, bedding, and other forms of fabric. The only downside to this type of storage appears to be if the bag splits, air can leak back in so your items are no longer vacuum-packed. Just be careful when handling them and avoid the bag becoming pierced by any sharp objects. A small pin prick might not be noticeable, but as time passes, air will slowly seep in.

If you can't find these bags in a local store, then search online where they can be easily purchased.

How to Clean and Organize Your Closet

If your home is cluttered, then it's likely your closet will need reorganizing too. The very thought of doing this may seem daunting at first, but believe me, once the process has started you will soon reap the benefits.

Next, remove all of the remaining items and sort them into individual piles. Use the surrounding floor space and bed to create separate areas for all of your t-shirts, sweaters, skirts, shirts, jeans, etc. so that each type of garment is grouped together.

Unwanted items of clothing should also be removed at this stage, along with any that no longer fit, are worn or have holes. Be brutal when deciding what items should go and ask yourself these three questions:

1) Do you love it?

2) Do you wear it?

3) Does it project the image you would like to be perceived by?

If the answer to any of these questions is 'no', then dispose of it.

When the closet is completely empty, and all of your clothing has been grouped together, you should wipe the closet out with a damp cloth and spray some kind of air freshener inside to clear any musty smells.

Look inside the closet to establish what space is available and think about what will need to go back in. The general rule here is that t-shirts, jeans, sweaters, and shorts will all need to be placed on shelving or in drawers within the closet. Boxes can also be used to store clothing that has been folded and if space is limited, using ones that stack easily on top of each other will help.

Items such as dresses, suits, trousers, and shirts (basically items that crease easily) will need to be hung on a rail, so ensure that you have enough hanging space available. If you are short of hanging space or shelving, then address this issue before putting anything back in.

If the closet is small, then consider splitting it into sections. This can make it seem bigger as well as help to keep things organized. Designate these areas for specific items of clothing.

It's always a good idea, when putting your clothing back into the closet, to store them depending on how often they are used. Keep the frequently used items in an easy to reach place, and the least needed somewhere less accessible. Try installing additional areas at the top and bottom of the closet to store those rarely used garments. Consider using hooks inside the closet to give additional storage space for coats and jackets.

Now would be a great time start to using the 'Hanger Trick' that we previously discussed in an earlier chapter. This would help you to continue weeding out any unused clothing. Another good tip is to set aside a time to manage your closet once a month with a full de-clutter twice a year. It is often said that, the best times for doing this is at the end of a season or an important event.

How to Organize a Teen Girl's Closet

The actual process of organizing a teenage girl's closet should not differ too much from any other, but it will probably involve more work due to the amount of clothing involved. In addition, you will probably encounter problems with getting her to continuously maintain this.

I'm assuming the teenage girl will be present if you are de-cluttering the closet, so let's try to make it as fun as possible by playing her favorite music. The next step is to apply some basic rules that she can follow with minimal effort. These should be the same as before, which were to discard any unwanted items, put any dirty washing in the laundry bin, and then sort the remaining items into groups.

Consider the space available in the closet and use simple but creative ideas to help store as much as you possibly can. Extra inside shelving with baskets and small boxes are great for storing handbags, purses, and belts, whilst an additional rail can provide valuable hanging space for dresses and coats. When purchasing storage boxes to use in the closet, consider buying clear/see-through containers because these will make life easier when looking for things she wants to wear.

A shoe rack may also be useful and this can be kept in the closet or elsewhere. An alternative to the conventional rack is a shoe organizer that can be hung from the back of a door. These come with pockets in which the shoes can be slipped into, so freeing up valuable space.

Try storing jewelry in a box or in an organized draw and try to keep colored items together because these will inevitably be worn at the same time. One of those cheap fishing tackle boxes can be great when used as a jewelry box.

The key to keeping the closet organized is to make sure that each garment has its own section and all of the accessories have their own storage box.

Every six months make a point of asking the teenager to go through the closet to sort out anything that has not been worn for a while then encourage her to get rid of these items. Similarly, get her to remove any out-of-season clothing and store them in a less accessible place like the loft or garage.

The chore of maintaining the closet won't seem so daunting to your teenager if it is kept manageable between the larger de-cluttering exercises. Help her along by complimenting her whenever she organizes or clears it out it herself. Try to make her feel good about what she has done because the outcome will be of benefit not just her, but to the both of you.

How to Build a Closet Organizer in a Closet with Dormered Walls

A closet with dormered walls is likely to have less storage than a standard one but finding a ready-made organizer able to utilize this awkward space is virtually impossible. This is because most of the pre-built closet organizers on the market are designed with only the standard type in mind.

A solution to this problem can be to design and make your own purpose-built organizer. You can attempt to do this yourself, if you are confident in such matters, or you can enlist the help of a professional.

If you do decide to go down this route by yourself, then it is important to have the right tools. Take a trip to your local hardware store to buy the timber and make sure you have a tape measure, screwdriver, drill, and plenty of screws.

During the design phase, it is important to look at how best to utilize the space. The fact that you have dormered walls inside your closet will mean that one side will be deeper than the other. For the purposes of this exercise, we will assume that the sloped wall is to the side of the closet and not at the back.

To use the space effectively, it's always a good idea to try and break it down into different areas. Think about the best place to put a hanging rail because you will probably need to position it in the tallest part of the closet to provide adequate clearance. This would usually be on the opposite side of the sloping wall. Consider inserting a piece of timber that divides the closet from top to bottom. You could also attach shelving on the other side between the timber and sloped wall.

If the thought of designing and constructing your own organizer doesn't appeal to you, then consider using a professional. Ask friends and relatives to recommend a good carpenter or handyman, then contact them for a quote. They will, probably, need to come round and look at the closet before quoting. They may even be able to suggest a few ideas if you are struggling.

How Much It Approximately Costs to Have a Professional Design an Organized Closet

The cost of designing an organized closet will really depend on factors such as size and the amount of detail involved.

If you are looking for a basic design, for a relatively small area, then you should expect to pay for materials plus one to two days labor. Assuming that the design is fairly straightforward, then I would estimate that you should be paying anything from $400 to $600 (equivalent to approximately £250 to £400 for British readers). Please note, this is only a rough guide based on the cheapest timber-frame option.

On the other hand, if you are looking for something a bit different, the cost of your closet may run into the thousands. At the top end of the design-range many, people choose to have walk-in closets that effectively act as a separate room. These will incur additional material and labor costs simply because of their size. Sometimes, lighting will need to be installed and checked for compliancy against electrical regulations. As a rough estimate, expect to pay anything between $3000 and $5000 for a top-of-the-range walk-in closet that provides 50 to 80 square foot of closet space.

Simplicity and Harmony

Maintaining an organized home will be an ongoing procedure – it will never stop! It's important to remember this because, as long as you have possessions, there will always be the threat of clutter. Not allowing it to get out-of-hand is the key to success and implementing a few simple rules, such as the ones I have discussed, will help to ensure this.

Reclaiming your life so you are not ruled by your possessions will go a long way in providing you with a simplified lifestyle. Learning to detach will not only result in your home becoming bigger and better but will also give you a sense of pride and satisfaction. Your home will be easier to clean and organize. It will become a calm, pleasant place away from the hustle and bustle of the world outside. Your home will have become your own personal oasis.

Are you ready to begin?

About the Author

Judith Turnbridge is a married artist with an interest in interior design. She enjoys painting, calligraphy, and caring for her garden. Her two children have now grown up and flown the nest, and the two hungry mouths she now feeds belong to her two fluffy cats.

Other books by Judith Turnbridge:

Super Simple Home Cleaning: The Best House Cleaning Tips for Green Cleaning the Home

The Super Simple 30-Day Home Cleaning Plan: Making Time to Beat the Grime

How to Organize Your Life to Maximize Your Day: Effective Time Management Tips and Ideas to Simplify Your Life

Out of Sight, Out of Mind: Easy Home Organization Tips and Storage Solutions for Clutter-Free Living

Nature's Miracle Elixir: The Essential Health Benefits of Coconut Oil

How to Survive a Disaster: Emergency Preparedness for You and Your Family